T0108906

THE LIFE OF A HUNTER

KUHL HOUSE POETS *edited by Jorie Graham and Mark Levine*

POEMS BY MICHELLE ROBINSON

The Life of a Hunter

UNIVERSITY OF IOWA PRESS   IOWA CITY

University of Iowa Press, Iowa City 52242
http://www.uiowa.edu/uiowapress
Copyright © 2005 by Michelle Robinson
All rights reserved
Printed in the United States of America
Design by Richard Hendel

No part of this book may be reproduced or used in any
form or by any means without permission in writing from
the publisher. All reasonable steps have been taken to contact
copyright holders of material used in this book. The publisher
would be pleased to make suitable arrangements with any
whom it has not been possible to reach. This is a work of
poetry; any resemblance to actual events or persons is
entirely coincidental.

The University of Iowa Press is a member of Green Press
Initiative and is committed to preserving natural resources.

Printed on acid-free paper

Library of Congress Cataloging-in-Publication Data
Robinson, Michelle, 1979–.
Life of a hunter: poems / by Michelle Robinson.
p.   cm.—(Kuhl House poets)
ISBN 0-87745-952-5 (pbk.)
I. Title.   II. Series.
PS3618.O333L54 2005
811′.6—dc22   2005041768

05 06 07 08 09 P 5 4 3 2 1

Sometimes he could hear Crusoe speaking, as though through a tape recorder, with his own voice: "I drew up the state of my affairs in writing; not so much to leave them to any that were to come after me, for I was like to have but few heirs, as to deliver my thoughts from daily poring upon them, and afflicting my mind."

— The Human Factor

It was a nice write-up. It gave the impression that Geiger had been killed the night before, that Brody had been killed about an hour later, and that Captain Cronjager had solved both murders while lighting a cigarette.

— The Big Sleep

CONTENTS

v

ACKNOWLEDGMENTS

The following poems were published in *Conjunctions* (43): "From this miserable mutineer a stutter, / For when we are reading Dostoevsky in caves.," "This may or may not become a permanent position.," "Keith," "I'd like to take leave of these things, and try / the harness again. It wouldn't be difficult.," [untitled] ("Everything beyond Florida Ave. . . ."), "This passenger is one of three conspirators.," "Currency," "Pepper," "Aberration," "Clothes for the body that expands," "Much was lost and gained en route.," "When Smithson looked into the Salt Lake what he saw," "There Being Transfer," [untitled] ("We bought a coat hook . . ."), "He could have wrapped up his eyes and thrown them away.," "The narrator dismembered the corpse and hid the parts in 3 sections," "There Being Transfer." The following poems were published in the *Colorado Review* (Fall/Winter 2003): "Clothes for the body that expands," "From this miserable mutineer a stutter, / For when we are reading Dostoevsky in caves."

I

In his dreams, it is always the other people who are naked.

The curtains in his room give the appearance of a mirror.

A man on the street smokes an unsharpened pencil.

"If I can make it to the end of the street
with my eyes closed, tell me everything

will be okay." This shirt is worn
by an eccentric male character. Max is different,

he does not find the love of others disgusting.
Not Jen, terrible, sweet, she liked to give her hand

up the ass. We are told this is the way things are done
on Wall St. Max seemed to think Jen smelled funny

of course he's right but who's pegging him? I know
he is thinking about this, and possibly small things,

like the man who walked by a stroller outside the T and went
back down to wave at whatever it was that was inside.

Or else, the way things mean less cinematically,
mean even less than before. The shirt —

No guest, however obstreperous, is ever asked to leave.

"So perhaps I am only pitiable, or more likely absurd,
like the boy I heard of who was allergic to grass

        The way my thoughts and her body dovetailed.

        The way I am neither invented nor made by hand.

        The way I am modifying.

FROM THIS MISERABLE MUTINEER A STUTTER,

FOR WHEN WE ARE READING DOSTOEVSKY IN CAVES.

How can I describe to you the sadness of my precision?
I am Brendan, owner of dictionaries,

Whose intoxicating contents leveled me with one blow.

In Stockton, a fellow looked at me. We threw down right
there, behind a Mexican grocery store.
I pummeled him until the grease poured from my fingers.

Ah fuck it all sometimes!
I thought truth would speak from that thing that is
physical. I am wrong.
I want it on my grave:
                    I am wrong.

Whose product follows me, that ghost.
The scuffling sounds of dusty sneakers and sheets flapping. His constant
clumsiness!
["Don't leave me now. I can't get through this night without you."]

I pummeled him until the grease poured from my fingers. My —

(Has it been a hoax?

The man on Belton Street selling poetry. The man who laid hands on him.
The sandwich board for Johnny's Luncheonette.
And Damrosch, that quick-witted kitten, who will make me laugh anon!)

My fellows!

How can I persuade you of the imprecision of my sadness?
I have forgotten to take this body off

Whose letter ends, "I don't know what to write.
I don't know what you want to read. Not this."

KEITH

His name is Nick. He is the guy at Vicki's housewarming party
who tells me how to make cocaine in my bathtub.
He looks like this guy on the cover of *The Snarkout Boys*
and the Avocado of Death (in the book he is Walter Galt
and his father is a sausage manufacturer). In this poem he is
the guy who leaves a note in my pocket.

There is a note in my pocket.

I feel like I'm shuffling through this, the fatness of it.
Let me explain:
>   Here is when Nick leaves the note in my pocket.
>   The note says Nick — the guy from Vicki's housewarming party.
>   Call me.
The note means this:
Nick was the name Nick gave when the name Nick
gave was a variable assignment for Nick.

Here there is a break in the pattern;
After this I will refer to Nick as Keith only.

>   "Play out the play" (II.iv.490)

Last night I slept with a belt around my neck.

I say to Keith, "Nick, you must have spilled
Something on your shirt." Keith says, "This is not beer.
I just don't bathe." Keith smells like beer.
Keith talks like something beautiful.

We are eating red Jell-O. There is not a note
in my pocket.

The next day I'm walking down the street Vicki says
who did you sleep with last night I say this guy named
Shakespeare.

In the same way it is possible to believe
in the imaginary, we are thinking about each other
as if we are thinking about ourselves.

That matter should exhibit this behavior:
> My father is a blank and not a blank.
> I am a blank and not a blank.

So I ask him about it this morning and he says, "Bring it up in group."

"I cannot tell half of what I saw."

Should this suffer us to join together.
The things that hinge me to you —
We fret, and fret, and we are not altogether unhappy.

If there is a verb that means
unanchored and yet still, it would go here.

> "I cannot tell half of what I saw."
> "We wanted to know if we were good out there."

When we are here
> At once the sense of weightlessness and of slowness

this unexpected depth.

Is there room to enter side by side?

This may or may not become a permanent position.

That was striking to this goon's feeble mind.

When grammar hung itself from the rafters
they trussed me up like a chicken cordon bleu
and poured chemical insults into my body.

I was the scapegoat, the poor fish tank rustling
the wires and glass that braced my neck.
                              The creaks and screws
that carried me to the table. The fantastic whispers.

In some absent or some other terrain could I have purchased
this exorcism?

This glum November something I am trying to figure
myself into this world, its drab and marvelous bits, its secret
schedules.

All the strangeness and the beauty have been parceled into objects.

Don't misunderstand. It was the most cynical year of our era
and anything would have been better than to have been asked
to find something beautiful.

TENANT

His reserve forms like a scab. And the decision not to stop breathing — a lapse in the
architecture of things.

On the other side of the divide a road, and on this side of the divide a road.

They are perhaps the same road.

There, the footprints of the man who will walk
    either I am pushing my thoughts into order like a coiffeur or I am
    walking next to myself or
                         She throws her hands about his neck — "It's you I love!"
    this strumming — This is not love.

There will be terms like hostages: calm and sad, barefoot. For now, he will wear his
hand by his side.

He lies down on the wooden slats in a rehearsal of his own death. "I have the sadness
of getting out of bed," he says. "That's the saddest thing I ever heard!" the plump
man responds, bursting into tears.

I'm in a five by seven block in a block of five by sevens.

My first take was in the numbers at high stakes.

When a mark threw a fit, clutching my knees, I'd speak:
"Let the fool live, just to punish him."

I've baked blades into cookies. I've baked bread
into bread. I've rolled doughnuts in dentist quality cocaine.
Pumped them full of liquid ecstasy.
Joe, that meat-headed smuggler, stole my heart.

He was an eighteen-karat sissy. He pulled that trigger
and his face turned to gravy.

Gravy! Dad shopped himself around and ended up in a ditch.
Mom threw down two pair against a flush
and lost my hand. I swear the deck was stacked.

Tomorrow is my wedding day.

Machiavel! Upstart! I spit on his good Kentucky bourbon.
I hear he ripped off Carbury's for a cool million.

When I was fifteen and waiting for the pigs
to come, I heard the whistle of the ice-cream
man, someone was selling something as I sat
at the kitchen table, and when I put my head
on that table I heard a voice. . . .

"Could I be her chauffeur without learning fearful things?"
— *Orpheus*

The devil takes the trouble to learn how to speak
our language, and the sea — the sea is no longer
itself, after this; it doesn't give the "no" of "yes and no,"

      It is the sound of a man who knows he is going to die soon.

"I'D LIKE TO TAKE LEAVE OF THESE THINGS, AND TRY

THE HARNESS AGAIN. IT WOULDN'T BE DIFFICULT."

The first sheet, properly arranged, simply turns the body into a ghost.

                               When I grew
to inhabit that skin, it was corroded with slim lines of a deep color:
the flowers from that kimono etched into the flesh: a tag
attesting to its former owner.

The second sheet. The sensation is of a space that cradles you.

A sheet, obsessively rendering its surface.

      What heaviness is netted in this cloth,
heaviness not much swayed by wind.

Chandler would have someone say, "How can you talk
like that before breakfast?" Or "You might as well rend
your garments," which is my own invention, but in
his manner, I suppose.

Nothing to do but give your old self the slip.

A sheet. Your head is in a pail of water.

A sheet: You slap out your cigarette if you think someone is coming.

A sheet: Because you won't say anything, I will tell you everything.

[UNTITLED]

"We couldn't say to you we are not like that at all, we couldn't answer back.
Darling, don't you see you are inventing us?"
— The Comedians

Everything beyond Florida Ave. is below sea level, some of it is woefully
below sea level, so that if you walk up the 13th St. hill you hear hydraulics
plugging away to keep water out.
                              "Where we are there's no way to reconcile
the dead and the dead."

We'd fetch them from any gully the frame of a man throwed down.
We'd stick a wrench in the neck, crease it, get in one piece the mug
turned ugly by death's blow, score it with acid, and climb that 13th St. hill,
where a doc would press putty into the sockets with his thumbs, touch
the bone in search of some physical glitch, touch this
magnificently crafted vessel for its volume, figure the sense
of the cranium by the number of seeds that could be crammed
into its hold. That was no way, Or that was the filthiest way,
with our bare hands: get them to work for us to tell the story
we wanted told.

            "Darling, I've lost my head."
            Says the skull to the doctor — No,
no, (*soothingly*) it's just that the light in the entryway has fused.

"I shall fear not the dark but what's in it."

Here the wind off the river turns the earth too soft for cleats, and later
drives that dirt into grit so sharp it cuts skin.
"Without my body, I'll have some trouble
settling down. I'll tell my spirit to go off
into a corner — you won't have it. They tell me

15

I'll grow up, a classroom will pry itself open,
admit me, will bait my throat with words,
will call on me (*soon*) for the type of assistance
only I can provide.

PEPPER

when I am vigilant vigilant remembering the uncensored lines
of you, the stark creases in your hands
not unlike an intermission from madness, greasy and sublime,

yet everything I say is a trembling non sequitur

when you are so anxious for the end of the second act
and the beginning of the third

when I would cross my lover for a Hershey's bar
and you, loathsome, are intensely more rich, more sweet
but reticent, so if I am that source of inexhaustible yes
then yes is a dirty word

you want to scrape all the humor from this wound
and leave only frailty

Over a grilled cheese and tomato soup I felt the hook
of it in the small of my back. Little Buckle kept moving
the vegetables around on her plate.

I wanted to pull out a machine gun and hose down
the place, but Ma, who belongs to Situation as much as
Rage, wouldn't have it. We seemed so far
from God's irresistible ordering of reality.

We piled into the Buick and sped west. I knew the fellow
was right close behind us. I played dominoes with Little Buckle, and counted
her toes. There was nobody else on that road that night.

When Little Buckle fell asleep, I read the new Ashbery. His last few
have been forbiddingly academic. Works (as all works do) begin to talk
about one another.

At last we reached the Indiana border and poured
out of the car and staggered onto a field, trying to find our legs.

He can't catch us now, Pa crowed, hitching up his breeches. That's the law
of the International Time Zone.

We all set back our watches.

II

When Smithson looked into the Salt Lake what he saw
was not the thing itself but the possibility
of the thing: what had in its approach the possible
consequence of stepping off the land, and into the water
and for which he would be made fun of by name:
clown, you irrelevant, shit-eater, Rob — not
Rauschenberg who erased deKooning's drawing, nor
Mitchum who could not see the picture, could only see
the frame, nor Stoppard, nor Shakespeare, no sucker
of stones was Smithson, no rocket scientist, whose roughly
carted rock trucked out to the rim of the lake a makeshift
anachronism: sediment, and grew steadily into land
because he did not *faire un trou* but a rotary, a gift and

what will be sweet to remember: swirling into the Salt Lake
he, who could have said "Take this!" one miserable rock,
who could have said "here is something

beautiful for you," who said, who could barely say
"Someone turned on a faucet inside me"
when he and the world became acquainted,
and thus succeeded in maintaining its mysterious
and wonderful affections, his hand dipping
into the water, occasionally, after the sediment
he was not certain was underneath in the same way he was not
certain the water would not rise about him, and it did: I did not
know for a long time generosity was rare,
or if the world is not eminently just and fair it is
sufficiently so, don't blame me, Smithson,
you were duly exiled: in the film: you run along

the Spiral Jetty, the helicopter cranes
above you, and reaching the end of the curving land
you rest briefly, dizzy and gratified, and start back, you,
who could do nothing: having skirted your way
along the scaffold could do nothing but run back
but I will explain:

[UNTITLED]

"What do we deduce from this letter, Watson? Nothing much, except that Mr.-er-Montgomery Jones is not one of the world's best spellers, thereby proving that he has been expensively educated."
— Partners in Crime

Jones scaled up the side of the house to scramble in a window
he thought was open but was not, and then a housewife wielding
a rake encouraged him to leave. "Hey you! Hey you!" he cried,
"I'm not a burglar — I live here!" — although there was nobody at home

to confirm this position. Jones was virtually new to these arrangements;
continually high-fiving himself in the shower; a man of many
stripes who screamed daily "I discovered you!" to the city and engaged
in insalubrious dealings with hoods, adoring their hooded-ness,
which seemed to owe a lot to Greek prototypes. The city found him

simple, perambulatory, a cakewalk, ham and eggs, baby, a folly
of affectations he made it his own, and, baldy, if we are in the wrong
regarding our opinion about the rudeness of the human race, so much
the worse for us. Then we are the boors, preoccupied with the mundane,
waiting for things out of nowhere to end by adding up, intermittently,

as they did for this fellow, who disappeared into an automobile
and poured himself into one layer of clothing after another
until finally he attracted the attention of a policeman, since, unable
to control his passions, he had double-parked. To whom I offer toasts.

Why, for instance, just that morning had he awakened with a knife
in his hand and a sense of foreboding? I hoped I'd run into a character;
it seems fitting that his behavior falls into familiar patterns:
A caution and an appetite, who was out of his depth when
executing a fantasy, provided that we define our terms correctly.

In spite of his recent insomnia, we have had very few complaints from the man whose arm is fastened to the wall of glass behind him; and if his body has been stretched into the position it is now, well, he has hardly anyone to blame for it but himself.

The apparatus was fashioned by Alexander Calder, and is without affectation; the right arm spindles up above the body and into a steel vice, which cuffs, if I may use the expression, the arm to the glass.

The grip draws attention to his five fingers. He is otherwise quite unaccomplished; I've often noticed this.

Someone, perhaps you, drew his attention to the fact of the glass. "We are always two!" he whispered urgently.

Could it be that his voice is still there? His left arm has grown brittle from disuse, and appears to unravel from the shoulder. His hair is limp like wheat, and dust has wrought its way into his collar and cuffs. The tweed a bit brusque, perhaps, but it is of course possible that he has not always had this brutishness about him.

He hides his indifference less and less. Did I say

the difficulty of sleep

"I have ink all over my body"

"Now I know less and less about who I am or who anybody else is. This river reminds me of another river."
— The American Friend

"You have played many jokes on me!" This stiff lug
took off to the traffic light and there affixed himself
so that he dangled like a pendant.

MUCH WAS LOST AND GAINED EN ROUTE.

This man is something like a spy.
His eyes tilt closed like a doll's when he leans back.

He has a perforated plastic box and a bottle of fruit juice that splashed
on someone's subscription.

The apple he holds is half cored, half fleshy.

In the underground bus station some hand has scrawled
on the light casings and on the benches "this is not an exit."

There is a deep bell barely audible down here.

"You don't know me. We have murdered a man together. We are friends."

River of gratitude, River of unthinking, River of cold stones,
In a shooting gallery, a man makes a paper target flutter.

Years ago it was dug into this metal and left
to rust, but in fact the paint has yet to flake and with teeth-

crushing hardness it's like a strong arm
with a steady job. Pulled down only by the weight of a picture frame

or perhaps a towel, it speaks not so much
of inevitability as of guts, as if molded with

deliberateness. There are very few things as dull as that.
My grandmother also held things together.

They say the boy who put his finger in the dike
was forgotten almost immediately well he wasn't

but he is nameless.

HE COULD HAVE WRAPPED UP HIS EYES AND
THROWN THEM AWAY.

And there were fire stairs, collapsible ribs slippery
with the rains' residue, dripping like Cerberus' jaws,
spilling open and zigzagging downwards like a handyman's
measuring stick, tracing the figure of an upended seismograph and interrupted,
at regular intervals, by a gentle terrace. So that we could be evacuated
real quick! — like the tug on a zipper's pulls that spills out its dull
grey ammunition, and the metal frame was lodged to our residence,
declining unvaryingly; each viaduct neatly welded, each flight a sling
sprung up on the side of the building, each edge an engine
turned scallop, cleanly beveled and embossed with robust
criss-crosses whose surface presence suggested a single
efficient mechanism, each ladder heavier than anodized aluminum
and configured such that it appeared to have bolted
itself into itself, the spaces so flush, so cleanly fabricated
that the metal seemed to frame the air it made visible,
like the grappling with Riemann sums that makes matter
over what exists beneath a curved line, rather than above it.

Prometheus, that bird feeder, never knew this! nor did the bitch
that gave birth to him, a woman "cheap" in the vernacular,
who could have, scouring his face with spit and her thumb,
told him "Be satisfied! with this: man, a bridge to the earth,
a mountain route stripped of its decametrical mile markers" —
Would he have hankered for atomic power — a gift to which we were
providentially entitled, (rather than our enemies), for a short while?

One time you wanted to follow a fire truck,
and took an omnibus train into the country, where
you found one, gliding down the highway in the night

and got closer and closer to it, until your body
shook with the heaving engine you screamed:
"Look at me! Look at me! Look at me!"

THE SECOND WOMAN I LOVED DID SOMETHING WONDERFUL
FOR THE WORD PEDAGOGY

The things that are false clamor and accost us they say
"we are false but we are here" and "we are here"
they want a living wage O false things! O tumbleweeds! I long
for the corrugated surface of her it was tremendous
we ate smoked salmon for breakfast, as a matter of fact, it was
really something. That killer voice I'm nothing

you I could almost touch, you
who like a crate of Florida
oranges are full of sunshine
you wouldn't believe the way she looked at me!

I feel like Kerouac, trying to strangle
an epiphany from all this —
but oh jesus her kleptomania! Those legs legs legs etc!

me left gasping with four letters spelled out on my stomach
"The pleasure is mine," she said, "I assure you," and humming, walked away.

Gelman is in a tight fix.
A bear is sitting on his rifle, which is high drama
for the Adirondacks
but not uncommon.

Back in Yonkers, Dr. Sikorski is unimpressed. "Yeah, the meek may
inherit the earth but we'll see
how long they can keep it."
    So we postpone the exhibition. The notion that one can have all
    good things is common, unpalatable. Man is not by nature monogamous, or

"You are a victim of the rules you live by."

At the reception, Gelman blundered his way
into your heart. You found him irredeemably
wealthy. You were both post minimalist
                    and in you
                    this softness
                    immeasure-
                    able and
                    unexpected.

The domestic calm is
exquisite. Gelman returns
to his first love, etching
by intaglio. His work
is biomorphic.
He dreams of Lichtenstein.

but enough superlatives — there was only one
thing that could come between Gelman and
danger and that was his psychiatrist.

Dr. Sikorski is desperate, and seeks other places to hide.

ARRIVING AT THE LANDING ONE HAS CROSSED OVER
THE SUBJECT

Some mason shoved stone into an album
of identical descents, sheeted the top with snow, and
clipped my shadow in a dozen crooked fragments.
I won't be tripped by carpentry, I tried to dwell
upon it, too clumsy to look back. Odysseus, homeostasis —
the first whose brand declared his being, the latter ripe
with bureaucratic office: Give me dominion
over these depths, take me safely to some landing!
Much ink has been spilled. These steps, such as they are, are
made to follow and I descended, peeved and grim,
clutching the railing, when I discovered Brendan at the stoop.

Quoth the Gentleman: "My bathrobe sash was the cord
that wrested the Arctic; each crevice a hand lock
where a plane of polished wood curved past the brim
wrought by a vertical precipice.
The floor wax served as the ice sheet the conquest
of what slipperiness sent the explorer downwards,
his bottom smashed against the grain in a swift
succession of thumps he cried "Send up the alarm!" —
a series of identical thumps into the arms of his stern
Mother, who was prowling at the foot. For this he was stayed
in bed the following day while his family went to the beach,

nestling in that doleful trench, consorting with The Hardy
Boys. Look, Shakes, you can fill in the gaps but the gaps
are still there. That part I added but it's in
the spirit of the text. His mother laid him down
for a nap: You've ruined the shirt that was mine,

my favorite — a hole, growing into a shirt, cut
just below the sternum of a child, Pull down
the shades, Hide his face, the afternoon light,
Some part of him might rest.

Despite untempered idealism and a large bank account,
he could not live in peace with inanimate objects.
Unpremeditated love centrifuged the savant,

unleashed the coarse beast of adult cinema, the convict
of breeding. The fucking idiot — he hated the emotions that keep vertebrate
animals alert. Guilt unhinged the subject,

left a gelatinous mass on the snow, an ex-celibate
seeking self-asphyxia. It would take six men to move him
to a cot of noxious smelling pine, now a candidate

for capricious stone engravings and ingenuous explanations —
Now I find it is neither easy to be clever
nor clever to be easy. Some god-awful misquotation:

This: an epigraph that cannot be recovered.
This passenger, who mocks his own departure.

The pasta will be done in two or three minutes.

When we were choosing to be men, Jon said
"Amazing." With something of a straight face.

That really turned me on! I mean, somebody
else would have said "Fuck it" or even "Christ"
but not Jon, whose every action was an inhalation.

All his stories came from the summer. I can't think
about anything else.

He didn't look at home in the name he invented
for himself. He would try to refrain
from drinking. Or, to me: "Man, you've gone
and done it now."

The drink. (*Cautiously*)

This is off the record, of course; if it was me I couldn't stop
drinking, in fact I didn't for months and then there is
Jon, who doesn't understand anything but that he wants
to be a man.

The wanting.
The series of prior acts.
The being branded.
The buoyancy.

III

You and the devil make a pact; you will be taken to the world, to see it in marvelous detail. Only that if you have already been and do not remember, he will clip it from you.

And so it comes to pass that you travel. But instead of monuments and cathedrals, the devil takes you to stations, food joints, rest stops. These places are common; it is impossible to distinguish one from another, though you have frequented many. Nevertheless you stab at it, your nose twitching, tense. In a public toilet you catch a glimpse of yourself, leaving, but it is actually your brother. Frantically rummaging, you miss one answer after another. It is some time before your luck changes.

When you return home, your head jerks, tender from the bruising. Your slender fingers throb with the pain of these dreadful excisions. Your children no longer recognize you. Something rattles when you move.

Later, in your study, you carefully unpack the thin strips and prepare for their delicate re-assembly. Then you hold each frame up to the light, passionately studying; memorizing all that there is. *This won't happen again*, you promise, spit glistening on your jaw. *Next time I'll be prepared.* And swiftly glancing over your shoulder, you discover that the room is empty. Quite some time ago the devil left you to your own devices.

Your parents taught you to scrape together prayers.
You did what they said but not because they said it,
bowing your head to the ground like the dead blooms

of a camellia. You telegraphed perfunctories: take, keep,
bless. Your tongue sought something current.

                                        The way things are

now: even though you know that you are in you can't breathe
easy. Somewhere, hot steel is flying. It's not here.
Your family is safe. Feeling suddenly less

bearish, you are wondering how, in autumn, your neighbor
manages with her beat-up van, a great scar
spread across the windshield, where the glass shattered and

rayed out, and still, marvelously, guts away rain.
You can think of terms for this. You think these terms
are not yours for the asking. But you go ahead and ask.

Did we not listen properly
to the cries of pain when they arrived? Wasn't there
a color like the morning sky, and didn't we weep
at the color? Perhaps that was a movie.

If we are cold, this absence becomes us. Or if not, I am
still always imitating myself — I found out about this yesterday.

Remember the word you used to describe the spaces
people make in us: I think it was *candor*.
Or was it *breathless*? Even in
dreams I'm rusty; in any case, I don't believe it.

Another town — its own hooliganism and quick chess.
Another town, same night.

Word come from back East: "I felt no cold,
nor did I feel any worry or alarm."

I would rather not make this boast early.

The East flipped me for a bitch like an Indian nickel.
They toughened my blood and pumped my chest full of lead.
I was a yellow-livered billy-goat. I was just 23

and my name was mud. O the knee-shaking sweetness!
While my first self cursed and slobbered, my second self sought the holster.
"I felt no cold, nor did I feel any worry or alarm."

How is it and wherefore, my gun-slinging
ballerina, my bicycling six-shooter,
you should now seek your shadow?

My second self, my East — I've had with your fast women and lonely bootstraps.
Your cross-hatches have covered my body.
Come to me! Come drink with me. Come share my bath water.

CUL DE SAC

That truck gusted air so hot
it put cracks in summer's cut-up face.
Firemen pulled up to check the hydrant;
water the color of rust filled up the bathtub.

So long to the man who lost both legs to the cement mixer
and still went the way down 4th Street to church.
Sitting on Aunt Maude's old brown couch
I got mosquito bites all over my hands.

When you hear me tell of the ends of things
my breath hums and stills.
Would it be the same for old people?
Or are we just making conversation —

    "Today, our child left a flock of stick people in the road
    sprouting balloons with the words run me over."

Hanging around the meat market clubs, drinking beer,
People don't happen to me. Not even the good-natured lechers
who once sprang up to exorcise my flavor of queer.
They dressed me up as a business man and I liked it. I endure
it. Now I have cufflinks and an attack of optimism; the allure
of stumbling so far towards propriety, and still it's the same
dirty joke. My mother has a hyphenated name.

I hitchhike west with my low-maintenance friends,
delinquents; they take all their jokes from the pages of the New Yorker.
They like cheap liquor and prepackaged food. But it ends
unhappily, lost on the New Jersey Turnpike (and here I hock
my fetish for respectability to beg for a meal). I am stalker-
crazy for street life.
                    Oh that je ne sais quoi de besoin! That taste
of sleep in my mouth, the delicious complicity in the fast pace.

[UNTITLED]

"There is a sort of fatality that pursues me."
— Cards on the Table

A band of history terrorists destroys all
evidence of the present tense. What will speak
first to the age that was waiting before? It's dog
tags all for those who skimmed the time off the heels
like molasses or crude oil; when the tongue slips
a ski mask jumps out from behind a bush.
Different things are now true, truth lying in general
where tragedy lay when he sensed the special reading
of a text he had written: Your uniform no matter except
which side of the grass you're on; Your dead used
to wring round the space where acts wrenched time
to being. If you could get behind it and see past, I
think, time would be only the husk of things, a coffin
wheeled on a gun carriage, the curious framing
that sustained the right to react against the presence
of another. What will commit all this to memory?
We will scout ahead ourselves — I feel as if I am already.

"Not all city life is modern; but all modern life is city life."
— Zygmunt Bauman

LIVING

We live in the city! The homes, the public squares
thrown up like new accidents, luminous and

the bikers in the life jackets, and the thrilling routine!
I guess that's what you'd call loss. One ends

by following a stranger, even until dark.
The package of clothes that sidles up! *Sweetheart* —

he calls me sweetheart — *how can I get to*
Mount Auburn? This grid is embroidered as sweetly

as lace; the streets spread like flowers.
Mother, such a dull mark as I, how can I clutch

at the grey cityscape? I'm supposed to report to a man
after breakfast, but the city is towing me

elsewhere, after a caterpillar of children, who cross
the street wedded to each other.

IF WE ARE "IT" FOR ONE MORE MINUTE THE GAME WILL HAVE BECOME BOTH BORING AND CRUEL

Let me give you an analogy: how I just spit
an ice cube back into the glass, which is something

even I was taught never to do. How what I can't decide is if
all impressions are incidental. Do you like feel it,

these grim rib-rattlings? Andrea, this morning, howling, *No one will ever
hire me because I have flaky dandruff!* Our friend Ralph

in another car accident; *She was somewhere between
a bimbo and a twit!* He's still shaken up.

One of these days — but you can tell his heart isn't in it.
You know the type: whoever's wrong has to do the supper dishes.

How tonight we cast lots for it. How it plays out tonight
I end up with you, but good grief let's not get emotional.

How you toss me the last of the beers. How you say you
don't like the stuff, but I know you always drank it before.

[UNTITLED]

I am very tired right now.
Do you know how difficult it can be?
The waking up stays with me all day.
I'll never be good again.
I don't have time for this.
(gesturing to face) This is why I look as if I died;
ah yes, this is the signpost of something.
The smell of cotton sheets streams from the laundry,
The sounds in my throat last night.
The young men were dancing in the Sukkoth all morning.
Night chafes the air like sandpaper.
Plainspeak? The solemnity of a poem.
This is not a secret. This is a conversation.
Should we be candid rather than clever?
How can I unfasten what is quiet?
The fact of being alone is not forgotten.
When you don't speak there is silence it has this grammar.

IV

EPILOGUE

Is it you who carries the end of things
you as close as my breath to me?

If fingers tumble across this seam
will they rake up words to describe it?

What fine thread scars over the ends of fingers
unfolding a most intense fulfillment?

Will they find this perfume foreign
who are not as close as I am to you?

[UNTITLED]

"Oh, my dear friend, when a girl is nervous it usually means a young man, not crime."
— *Death in the Clouds*

My lover is a flourish whose palms fall open she covers
My love covers her palms with white and smears the stuff
on her cheeks and eyes. My love uses a solution
that takes the canvas from the calligrapher and lights it
into a fluid until the fibers crack and flake and are interred
with turpentines and oils in an oak cask and siphoned
through a silver needle into a plastic bottle it is liquid
paper and my lover is its flourish.

Clementine, listen: when you cry real tears you will sleep
with the fishes. Put your ear to the water you will sleep.
My love is made of paper I will write in ink, my love
you will find love where you look for it look for it
in the bottle, spill the bottle on your face. When she behaves
herself my love is not for pleasure, but rough to the touch
like paper, and trembling until she spills the bottle.
My dear friend, I am bourgeois and see sin everywhere but
in my lover, who covers her face with her hands.

My love you are as flimsy as paper, I will trace you
on the wall and on the floor so that you will have a shadow,
I will tie bricks to you so that you have some comfort.

Even this (your brief absence) gnaws at me.
Autumn falls like a heavy bitch.
A dark imperative siphons joy.

When you say "I struggle" it's the novelty of independence,
the series of swift accidents and empty billfolds.
A dial tone wails like cardiac arrest.

Christ. If humans were capable of happiness,
that brief jolt of anesthesia,
instead of the cold tenderness of interruption . . .

My new my drowsy riddle has no sense.
She is asleep here, in this bed, here in this stopped moment,
this pattern-break, cosmic-joke, smug confected axiom

I moan, later.

You used to think you were Raskolnikov
on the pillow, crying and spewing blood,
a hunger artist propelled by your coughs,
starving all the time. I was very rude
and asked you to swallow. You didn't flail,
but let the barbed fingers, dirty hands claw
at your stained tunic. You were so frail.
The action changed when you were broke and raw
you fast became a method-acting junkie,
selling bold martyrdom down by the river.
Everyone clings to your voice like money
now, everyone listens when you whisper.
I've stifled my thoughts the whole world over;
you'll soon find that street people make poor lovers.

SYMPTOMS

I had vague, stirring dreams of culmination
on the flight to Bangkok, suffering the coarse
grasp of a limp, sexless mannequin
whose limbs were flushed, as if dispensing grace.

Bodies, litter, the freeway. Club Narcissus
maps the contours of angels, skeletal
waifs doubled over with appetite, loss
neon smoke, the stale sweat of arms, the sale.

Scowling, the driver tries to cheat us. His ethics
lack the fury of western honor, that thin flint
voice. We bypass the mechanics
of bargain and stagger away.
                              I am sent
mirror-rapt, shod with the reverence of mass
knees bent, still, watching this world undress.

There is never any physical action
that happens without our wanting
less. We apprehend the world in its littleness, because
there is a lack of metaphor, and because
this quiet that is unquestioned is always.

The arrival of night is something
you and I take for granted. This the trust we take
with some confusion. How your shoulders can
fit into my arm, how there is nothing
other than undressing, also,
than undressing is what we do.

The absence of intermediate pause
is evolution, this gnawing at the leash,
down to the flesh-bitten and the flesh
scrambling to contain everything that is coarse:
I found something hideous in the garden
today, these pieces of pottery, splinters
that had names on them but they were not ours.
They're human bandages, duty stricken
us when we stopped at the gas station
I can't get my mouth around this script
cop the john ate tugged on suddenly
your skinny arm, finding this constant work bitter,
"There's something wrong with the skin on this fruit,"
I said, ripping it with my teeth, "come closer."

FALLING INTO A RUG

Does my toppling into this driest expanse
divest my knowledge of thirst?

So near to my mouth these tepid fibers
is it your wool sweater I inhale?

Could this friction, this mild warmth singe
an exquisite sonata into my bare skin?

Will it rasp like a parched grass-whistle
roughly grazing my arm-front?

[UNTITLED]

There are certain kinds of breathing.

I fetch you: Isn't that
The rabbi who's been
Fucking around?
                    Wouldn't Your
Mother want to know.

Carlton used to say
every seven minutes
there's a break
in the conversation. Now

he holds up seven fingers.

Seven minutes later.
Again.

He made a gesture with his bare
hand, painting a picture of him-
self in the air.

Maybe he was pointing: Isn't
that
The rabbi who's been fucking around? Wouldn't
you
want to know, you

this huge thing
a sad pant
spooning I
summon you:

(*with feeling*)
>   lilatov
>   lilatov
>   lilatov
>   lilatov.

The methods of science are situation specific.

SATURNALIA

like a 12-gauge repeating shotgun, I muster a campaign
haphazardly, firing brash embraces from the canon of comic maneuvers
crushing my arms against you like a corset

something in this mongrel brand of possibility,
a permanent exhibition of spring, bright and wounded,
wrenches blood-lust ammunition from the un-mown grass,
the lunging sun, this carnivore

you capture all this in a sneering gesture,
stroking my teeth with the tips of your fingers.

Everything to do with happiness is so cloying,
and still so brittle, so easily fractured by an unrehearsed moment.

This is the germ of confession: your apologetic horror,
fainting with disgust, as we grow malignant and restrained.

And then, your leisured epiphany, the end to your professional illiteracy.
For us, who live together, there is no free verse.

You cannot resist an exit line:
"It dawns on me I am attending a wake."

It is not only a joke that we carry papers
in our own defense. These were us. Awkward to say
I am not them. So we are struggling into ourselves,
and it is even more insignificant than the way we feel about it.

And I will begin again. I am looking at you,
Our hands folding and your superb teeth —
What untranslatable witnesses! What if we could carry each other?

V

THE NARRATOR DISMEMBERED THE CORPSE AND HID THE PARTS IN 3 SECTIONS

You don't have to believe this. But I have no choice.
I live in the back of an elevator, for Christ's sake!
All day mimeographing the words, limbing the dull
things about, filing them chronologically, smuggling my self
for crumbs. Why shouldn't I say things? I think if I explain,
but friendly-like: because I've failed to become the thing,
You are sniffing around, playing the argot, swimming
the witch. Perfidy! By this self, this corner,
sleeve to my soul, this body, I warn you, we will meet.

But I've got another problem on my hands, this body
what confessed, "We didn't believe in the Bible
because God said to, we believed in God,
because the Bible said to." I didn't know
what to do! I clocked him, on account of him saying We —
that was the piece that delivered the sentence.
What can I do with the body? Look, my hands
are up, but you couldn't have otherwise expected me to be
still. Stale fucking cog! He was just another party,
waiting to be left. But you and I, we're riding together. He
didn't even know. He just happened to guess right.

[UNTITLED]

"Take it easy," says the Red Man. "Aw, drop dead," says the White Man. You see? There's your conflict. But the real conflict is between the White Man and the prairie.
— Leaven of Malice

We bought a coat hook, a two-pronged plate, and pinned it to the wall,
snug to where the doorjamb freed the wall. It was an arched metal rod
like a piece of taffy an assembly line had pulled, torquing it
with a dull spark, and flattening the end into a raindrop, spatulate,
like a miniature shoe horn. In the plate two holes were punctured,
and we fit into the holes two screws that thread it to their margins,
and ground the screws into the pilot holes that the drill bit made,
twice, so that the walls seemed to offer auscultations, suddenly
proffering a crooked finger, and another finger, the shape the hand takes
not having offered but having flung something: a curveball, a bowling ball,
the wrist wrenched to its extremity and the thrust, not like that usual
profligate, nor in the liberal dispensation of that hallowed signifier: Mother,
but the hand that coaxes a bow across a viol, as in Rosenmüller's Sonata 7a.
Though with its prongs no music, so when we pinned it to the wall,
inducing entrance, that he may take off his hat, or his coat
or anyhow another hook to a man should he want to hang something
who enters here, the wall was transformed, dangling our garments
like jowls, or perhaps our assembly nearer now to finished than we first believed: Men

      tugged two sheets of plaster over to a corner and built that corner: Men

      slammed two planes together, each shoving the other upright: You Men

      are the first models from which others are copied.

In the photograph, everyone is in
Suits and ties and tablecloths, all decked out
in grim splendor, the over-worked Helen
another captive, sophistries cloying at her throat.
The occasion is immemorable but not
the age, its function, how coolly the postmodern jackass
is received: "Hell hath no fury . . ." writes David Foster Wallace

thirty years later. Now, it is the pressure
of delivery wrenching Helen's face into the pained
expression that must pass for interest,
intent on tenure, immunity, to be no longer just dammed
labor! Helen peers over the gilt
frame at the clock, face colored by the kind
of influenza new mothers get: when it is still
biology and not yet art that hurts.

The end of the pre-atom bomb era gives birth
to the subject. First, she possesses her self, next
her self disclosure. Poetry blows breath
into her; it turns her on before it can turn
on her — her command comes from secret studies,
her power grows. Her detractors are obviously insane,
although lucid. If she is no poet but a studied critic,

most of us are bored by this esoteric distinction.
She plays ball like a pro.
                                        She can swallow a fly
from left field and slug it home.
                                        O household god
who answers to the name of Helen, we are yours!:
disciples, fans, captives, thieves. You, Maker
of the marvelous, open your cabinet of wonders!
Have us! Have at us! Let us say, "We were had!"

Like a stray dog, she approaches all things
at angles; sweeping the hair from her face,
a python gesture. That towel hangs
at her insistence.
                The old tub is all rust
and cracked skin, white but not as white as her
hidden skin, Hopkins and Harlequins,
the plastic scraps that say never burn

unattended. Helen in the bathtub
has arms as thick as a juice glass, has smoke
and steam keening to her face. It cools
slowly. When the flame vendles, the must
of damp paper and steel taper back.
If Helen rises, dripping, it is too late
to wound the wax and water,
                     the wet wick.

This way: her shoulders curve like an embrace,
spine bent. This angle: she looks past her body
into the fridge. A tub of cottage cheese,
unexpired; the clustered condiments, Land
o Lakes subtly spaced; slotted shelves pressed
up against a metal canvas.
                                        There are threads of dried honey
on the Formica, which she scuffs with her wrist.

Since yesterday, rings of Chianti have fused
to the countertop. Helen with her thumb
against the spine of a wineglass, lips pursed,
seamless. Helen wrests open the tight
screwed sink. Helen, who will sponge
the round and heavy rimmed insults, scouring
until the soapy water has overtaken her sleeve.

LET US NOT EXPRESS OUR LOVE IN CHILDREN:

A painting by Barnett Newman.
No, a lithograph by Barnett Newman.

In division, there is symmetry. In replication,
there is the embarrassment of having a body.

There is the embarrassment of having a body.

They won't let us be single. They think.
They don't have to think. They don't have terms.
They watch. They don't have to watch.

Am I a part or am I an other? you
were saying. Is that anything, now? I am
impatient, I am fighting sleep. I am
looking at these words, and it isn't possible.

In spite of his recent insomnia, we have had very few complaints from the man whose arm is fastened to the wall of glass behind him.

If his body has been stretched into the position it is now, he has hardly anyone to blame for it but himself.

The apparatus was fashioned by Alexander Calder, and is without affectation.

The right arm spindles up above the body and into a steel vice, which cuffs the arm to the glass.

The grip draws attention to his five fingers.

He is otherwise quite unaccomplished, I've often noticed this.

Someone, perhaps you, drew his attention to the fact of the glass.

Tick into the floor map the perforations that signify depth,
And you will have invited the apparatus to appear, the stairs,
that instrument that connects one level to another by way of
a run of curbs, squares of a sidewalk lugged atop one another,
cement planks reflexed into an angle that ascends harmoniously —
This is why I became a Trigonometrist! that pleasure, as
Upwards and Over trade fours for several measures,
seeming to fulfill an equation of liturgical importance,
the way the Rabbis thought each act of human sin coaxed God
to remove himself to a layer of heaven that was more distant,
that great leveler like an umpire's thumb signifying some lapse
in conduct or in skill, and entertaining for a long moment the prospect
of favoring the opposition: their measly Rhetoric, their kulchah
their immodest and untenable admiration of the naked human body,
and then, those who were inclined toward industrial time, or time
associated with literacy, and this community evolved into a tangle
of wires that spread to the recesses, to the ends of the earth,
and even into the tenements, the slums, which we
now call more appropriately by the name of its etymological
cousin, the projects, and which we defend bravely,
not having the leisure to debate if it matters. Yes, it is
a bloody and mawkish line. Yes, you can sense the presence
of the heat, blue-collared and armed. Yes, one might be driven
to appropriate life if one is told the alternative is to "Stay here,

and wait for your own destruction," as Asaji informs Washizu
in the Japanese film *Throne of Blood*, Kurosawa's adaptation of *Macbeth*.
I came to this history through the back door, and it is a movement
that, once completed, leaves one winded. But the interpretation
of a thing, built into space with much resolve, is what I will report:
it is not by tapping on it, for instance, that one discovers
whether it is empty, or whether it is safe, or whether it is sound.

Poring through piles of unlearned trash, climbing
the margins of your ego, I spent
no earth shattering moments of joy, discovering:

Each smile, each thought of each smile, each movement
was a warped exercise in claymation,
a slow fumbling murmur of discontent.

We built crude electronic constructions
inside us, thinking somehow it would be hotter
there, harsher. I traded cheap conversation

for your thoughts, ceding to you self-slaughter.
The thought of burning flesh made my mouth water.

Not satisfied with the return of this agony, I traveled
for some time and soon realized I had seen
nothing, only wrestled with the elements,
had not grasped the wholeness of the world. I fell in
with a man whose stories I longed
to tell, who lived decently in another part
of the country. It is one thing to be many
miles from you, I wrote, but there is another
difference that is not unspeakable. I should
have realized it would be the same for him;
he would clutch me in bed and plead Come
with me. Come with me. It couldn't possibly
have mattered. He had committed
his grandfather to a home in Alabama.
The old man scattered flour making pancakes,
and would sing every morning. Even for us,
that is, you and I; that our houses suggest
plumbness, perhaps — though how would we have
them show us ourselves? Things are
flimsy, as we are. There is nothing
analogous to this, or if there is it would be in
Kurosawa's *Red Beard*, Mifune rescuing the child
from the brothel, and, looking at the litter
of men and bodies he has broken,
shakes his head, noting sadly, "This is not
how a doctor should behave."

Now, and it is still
raining, my child speaks
over the rumbling
locomotive. The cars
are clawing their way up the slick street.

My child speaks and I let
rain bury in his shoulders.
When his head cranes back, my great paw
catches the start of his spine.

My child speaks, my face
ginger-raw and bald, smelling
of the damp train. It cannot be
that he sees me as I am.

The little hand clings to the pole in the train.
Your wet hair is dripping in my hand, my boy.
There is the sound of turned-over earth.